Communication Skills for Leaders

Delivering a clear and consistent message

Fourth Edition

Bert Decker

50-Minute Manager™

This 50-Minute Manager™ book is designed to be an excellent workbook for self-study as well as classroom learning. All material is copyright-protected and cannot be duplicated without permission from the publisher. *Therefore, be sure to order a copy for every training participant through our Web site, **50minutemanager.com.***

Communication Skills for Leaders

Delivering a clear and consistent message

Fourth Edition

Bert Decker

CREDITS:

President, Axzo Press:	**Jon Winder**
Vice President, Product Development:	**Charles G. Blum**
Vice President, Operations:	**Josh Pincus**
Director, Publishing Systems Development:	**Dan Quackenbush**
Developmental Editor:	**Steve English**
Copy Editor:	**Ken Maher**

For more information, go to www.logicaloperations.com

Printed in the United States of America
1 2 3 4 5 08 07 06

Table of Contents

Appendix 93

About the Author

Bert Decker is a nationally recognized communications expert. The company he founded, Decker Communications, Inc., has been training hundreds of thousands of people for decades, recognized for over 20 years as one of the leading communications training companies.

Decker Communications provides communications consulting and skill building to more than 400 major organizations. The Decker Method™ is recognized as the best in its field for enhancing communication performance.

Bert Decker has also written the groundbreaking book, *You've Got To Be Believed To Be Heard,* has appeared on the NBC Today show several times as its communications expert, commenting on the U.S. presidential debates, and he authors the *Create Your Communications Experience* blog at www.bertdecker.com.

Communication Skills for Leaders is based on the Decker Method™ and may be used effectively with the popular book *Creating Messages That Motivate* on the Decker Grid™, available through Decker Communications and at www.deckercommunications.com. Decker Communications, Inc. is headquartered at 575 Market Street, Suite 1925, San Francisco, CA 94105, (415) 543-8100.

Preface

Christine Figari was a trainer with Decker Communications for nearly two decades. She first called me when the company was only a couple of years old and quite a bit leaner than it is today. "We're really not hiring new trainers right now," I said, "but go ahead and send your resume. We're always looking for good people."

I was working in my office the next day when our receptionist brought in Christine's resume and said, "I told her you wouldn't be able to talk to her without an appointment, but she insists on seeing you in person."

I scanned the resume and saw that it was good, but not spectacular. I thought this was a little pushy, but figured I ought to be friendly at least, so I walked down the hall. I found Christine to be much more impressive than her resume.

What really struck me was her certainty—energetic voice and manner, great posture, and authentic smile. She radiated confidence and competence. I learned more of what I needed to know about Chris within the first 30 seconds after we shook hands than from her entire resume.

We ended up talking for half an hour. Two months later, I hired her.

The point of this story is that personal impact *does* make a difference. Effective communication is critical in work and at play. It's particularly important to your professional effectiveness because of today's increasingly competitive environment.

This new edition of *Communication Skills for Leaders* explains the communication-leadership connection and includes updated examples to guide you in learning effective communication techniques.

Achieving excellence in interpersonal communications is a complex process made up of nine basic skills, which are presented in this book. You'll learn why each is important and will be able to practice the skills through a variety of exercises, assessments, checklists, and self-tests. You'll find yourself using your newfound skills dozens of times a day—both in business and in your personal life.

Many of the ideas are commonsense. Some are new. Most important, they all work. They've been tested and proven by hundreds of thousands of business executives, managers, and salespeople who've participated in the Decker Communications Communicate to Influence™ training programs.

Communicating is a learnable skill. It takes work, but the results are worth it. With practice, you can raise this skill to an art form and even enjoy the process.

Good luck!

Bert Decker

Learning Objectives

Complete this book, and you'll know how to:

1) Use the keys to effective interpersonal communication: Believability and the 9 Behavioral Skills of Communication.

2) Develop Connection with your listeners via the behavioral skill of Eye Communication.

3) Develop energy in your interpersonal communication via the behavioral skills of Posture and Movement, Gestures and Facial Expressions, and Voice and Vocal Variety.

4) Develop credibility in your interpersonal communication via the behavioral skills of Dress and Appearance and Language, Nonwords, and Pauses.

5) Develop interaction with your audience via the behavioral skills of Listener Involvement, Humor, and the Natural Self.

Workplace and Management Competencies mapping

For over 30 years, business and industry has utilized competency models to select employees. The trend to use competency-based approaches in education and training, assessment, and development of workers has experienced a more recent emergence within the Employment and Training Administration (ETA), a division of the United States Department of Labor.

The ETA's General Competency Model Framework spans a wide array of competencies from the more basic competencies, such as reading and writing, to more advanced occupation-specific competencies. The 50-Minute Manager Series finds its home in what the ETA refers to as the Workplace Competencies and the Management Competencies.

Communication Skills for Leaders covers information vital to mastering the following competencies:

Workplace Competencies:

▶   Adaptability & Flexibility

Management Competencies:

▶   Informing

▶   Clarifying Roles & Objectives

For a comprehensive mapping of 50-Minute Manager Series titles to the Workplace and Management competencies, visit *50minutemanager.com*

About the 50-Minute Manager Series

The 50-Minute Manager Series is designed to cover critical business and professional development topics in the shortest possible time. Our easy-to-read, easy-to-understand format can be used for self-study or for classroom training. With a wealth of hands-on exercises, the 50-Minute books keep you engaged and help you retain critical skills.

What You Need to Know

We designed the 50-Minute Manager Series to be as self-explanatory as possible. But there are a few things you should know before you begin the book.

Exercises

Exercises look like this:

EXERCISE TITLE

Questions and other information would be here.

Keep a pencil handy. Any time you see an exercise, you should try to complete it. If the exercise has specific answers, an answer key is provided in the appendix. (Some exercises ask you to think about your own opinions or situation; these types of exercises don't have answer keys.)

Forms

A heading like this means that the rest of the page is a form:

FORMHEAD

Forms are meant to be reusable. You might want to make a photocopy of a form before you fill it out, so that you can use it again later.

A Note to Instructors

We've tried to make the 50-Minute Manager Series books as useful as possible as classroom training manuals. Here are some of the features we provide for instructors:

- ▶ PowerPoint presentations
- ▶ Answer keys
- ▶ Assessments
- ▶ Customization

PowerPoint Presentations

You can download a PowerPoint presentation for this book from our Web site at *50minutemanager.com*

Answer keys

If an exercise has specific answers, an answer key will be provided in the appendix. (Some exercises ask you to think about your own opinions or situation; these types of exercises will not have answer keys.)

Assessments

For each 50-Minute Series book, we have developed a 35- to 50-item assessment. The assessment for this book is available at 50minutemanager.com. *Assessments should not be used in any employee-selection process.*

Customization

These books can be quickly and easily customized to meet your needs—from adding your logo to developing proprietary content. 50-Minute Manager books are available in print and electronic form. For more information on customization, see 50minutemanager.com.

Keys to Effective

Interpersonal

Communication

"The ability to express an idea is well nigh as important as the idea itself."

—Bernard Baruch

In this part:

- ▶ Believability
- ▶ Behavioral Skills

Believability

Most of us would agree that, in business as in all of life, the success of any presentation depends on the *believability* of the person speaking. Indeed, a person's believability is critical to any interpersonal success. No matter what's said, it isn't going to make much difference to the listener unless the speaker is credible and believed. Believability is the most significant factor to effective communication.

This isn't news to most people. What *is* news is how this elusive concept is rarely taught in school. Even more important, believability has yet to rise to the forefront of our minds as we engage in interpersonal communications in business; yet it's critical to our success.

We sell ourselves through communication. Whether we manage people, products, services or any combination of these, we're all selling ourselves. Our success is determined by our ability to communicate—to persuade our listeners to action. And our ability to communicate effectively is dictated by how we're perceived by our listeners. Therefore, the greatest investment we can make is in developing our communication skills, increasing our awareness of how we're perceived by others and improving those skills to achieve the impact we seek.

This book breaks down the intangible factor of *believability*, dissecting the whole package of *successful communication* into bite-sized pieces. It applies to public speaking, informal presentations, and the myriad of one-on-one interactions we engage in every day. Mastering interpersonal communication skills begins with building credibility and believability into everything we communicate.

Verbal, Vocal, and Visual Cues to Believability

Three elements are communicated each time we speak—verbal, vocal, and visual. The verbal is the message itself—the words the speaker says. The vocal element is the voice—intonation, projection, and resonance of the voice that carries those words. And the visual element is what listeners see—primarily the speaker's face and body.

UCLA Professor Albert Mehrabian, one of the foremost experts in personal communications, conducted a landmark study on the relationships among these three elements. He measured the differences in believability among the verbal, vocal, and visual elements. What his research found was that the degree of consistency among these three elements is what determines believability.

"I believe that a good leader does not set himself above the team."

BELIEVABILITY BROKEN DOWN

In the spaces provided, write your estimate of how much believability each of these elements conveys when you're speaking (interpersonal communication) to persuade a listener. The percentages should total 100.

Verbal	_____	%
Vocal	_____	%
Visual	_____	%
Total	**100**	**%**

Compare your responses to Professor Mehrabian's results in the Appendix.

Consistency = Believability

Professor Mehrabian's communications research, reported in his book *Silent Messages*, was based on what observers believed when an individual's verbal, vocal, and visual elements conveyed messages *inconsistent* with one another. When Mehrabian tested inconsistent messages, he found that the verbal cues were dominant only 7% of the time, the vocal dominated 38% of the time, and the visual cues were the primary carrier of trust and believability—a whopping 55% of the time.

If the message is *consistent,* then all three elements work together.

Consistency + Energy = Impact

The excitement and enthusiasm of the voice work with the energy and animation of the face and body to reflect the confidence and conviction of what's said. The words, the voice, and the delivery are all parts of a whole – a whole that must be integrated to convey a consistent message.

When we're nervous or awkward or under pressure, we tend to block our content and relay inconsistent messages. For example, if you look downward, clasp your hands in front of you in an inhibiting fig-leaf position, and speak in a halting and tremulous voice as you say "I am excited to be here"—you're delivering an inconsistent message. The words won't be believed.

When you're presenting your idea, you need energy to deliver your message into the heart and mind of every listener. Compare that with a rocket delivery system. There's the payload, or rocket ship, which a large Atlas or Titan booster rocket must launch into orbit. Without a strong, powerful booster rocket, it doesn't matter how well crafted the payload is, because it will never get there.

In communication, your message is the payload. If you're nervous or wooden, your delivery system will go awry and your payload won't be delivered.

Some people in business are like cannons ready to fire – like rockets with no payload. They may have great delivery skills but no verbal content. Others have detailed, brilliant ideas and productive things to say, but they block the delivery system to get it out there.

A large number of people in business give inconsistent messages. This inconsistency is probably the biggest barrier to effective interpersonal communications in business.

Making the Emotional Connection

Another barrier to effective interpersonal communication is failing to reach listeners' unconscious, *feeling* level. Extensive research has dramatized the importance of making this emotional connection. Indeed, it's a widely accepted principle of marketing and sales that people "buy on emotion and justify with fact."

Whether what you're selling are widgets or yourself and your ideas, whether your listener is one person or one thousand, if you don't connect with your listeners' emotions, you won't connect with them very effectively.

This is because of our two distinct brains—the *First Brain* and the *New Brain*. The First Brain is our emotional brain, which physically, and often unconsciously, directs our thinking brain, or what could be called the New Brain.

First Brain and New Brain

The First Brain consists of the emotionally powerful limbic system, which is the emotional center, and the brain stem, which provides immediate instinctual response. The First Brain is primitive, primal, and powerful. It operates at the unconscious level.

The largest part of the brain, the cerebrum, consists of a very thin layer of brain cells called the cerebral cortex. All conscious thought, including language and decision-making, takes place within this thin layer of brain cells—the New Brain.

All sensory input—sight, sound, touch, taste, and smell—moves through the First Brain first. The visual input from our eyes goes directly to the First Brain. Then it's forwarded to the thinking New Brain, which makes sense of it or interprets it. If the visual pathways aren't stimulated very much (no movement, eye contact, gestures, etc.), the information isn't passed on as readily by the First Brain to the New Brain.

The same thing happens with the sound of a voice. The audio signals go into the First Brain before being transferred to the New Brain. If the sound tends to be flat, monotone, or filled with distracting nonwords, the First Brain tends to shut down and filter the information that's passed on.

The First Brain is a lookout, a defense mechanism, a channel for communications that provides positive sensory input. The First Brain also controls and triggers other emotions—such as distrust, anxiety, and indifference—because of what it sees and hears unconsciously. The First Brain is your mind's gatekeeper. It's this primitive part of the brain that gives intuitive impressions.

Have you ever met someone you immediately disliked? That's your First Brain reacting instinctively to a warning or signal that you might not even be aware of. Have you experienced love at first sight? Again, this is the First Brain in action, making a quick, intuitive judgment.

It's the First Brain that decides what information to let into the more developed and reasoning New Brain. This is why you must make an emotional connection to be heard.

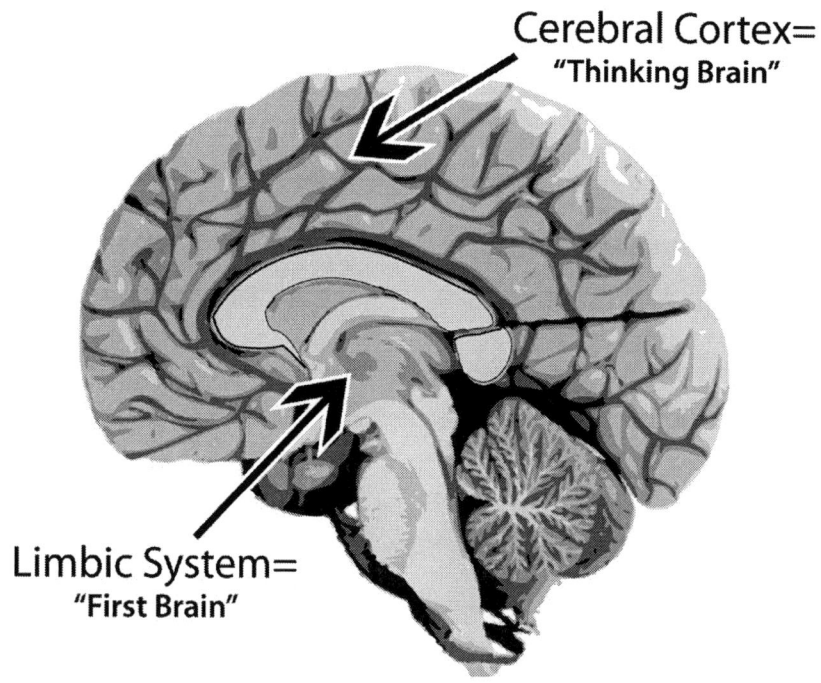

Cerebral Cortex=
"Thinking Brain"

Limbic System=
"First Brain"

First Brain	New Brain
Instinctual and primitive	Intellectual and advanced
300 to 500 million years old	3 to 4 million years old
Emotional	Rational
Preconscious/Unconscious	Conscious
Source of instinctive survival responses: hunger, thirst, danger, sex, and parental care	Source of thought, memory, language, creativity, planning, and decision-making
Common to many animals	Uniquely human

Believing What We Like

Whether our First Brain registers an instant like or dislike of a person we encounter, there can be little doubt that what it's responding to is something that person is communicating—verbally, vocally, or visually. No wonder likeability is a major component of trust. If we respond positively to people's communication, we tend to like them, and research shows we tend to trust people we like. Likeability and believability are intertwined—and both are dependent upon effective interpersonal communication.

Measuring the Personality Factor

The Gallup Poll has conducted revealing communications polls for all of the U.S. presidential races starting with the Kennedy/Nixon contest in 1960. This poll is conducted just two months before the presidential election. It asks for voters' preference in three areas—issues, party affiliation, and likeability, or "the personality factor."

What the polls have found is that the personality factor, scientifically measured by the Staples Scalometer, has been the only consistent predictor of the outcome of every one of the presidential races.

The Stanford Study

Professor Thomas W. Harrell of the Stanford Graduate School of Business completed a 20-year study[1] relating to career success. Although there were no "certain passports to success," Harrell found there were three consistent personal qualities that appeared to have a positive effect on the careers of those studied. These included:

- ➤ An outgoing, ascendant personality
- ➤ A desire to persuade, talk to, and work with people
- ➤ A need for power

Although interpersonal communication skills aren't necessarily related to the third characteristic, they're certainly intertwined in the first two. This is the same personality factor described above.

These studies and polls show that personality plays a major role in the effectiveness of your interpersonal relationships. Whatever you strive for, you can be sure that communication is the skill that will get you there. Luckily, despite what you may have read, you can alter your personality and change your communication habits to help you improve your interpersonal skills.

---

[1] Stanford University Study: Harrell & Alpert, March 1986

Behavioral Skills

Vocal delivery and the visual elements—as well as personality, likeability, and openness—are the primary ingredients of high-level interpersonal communications. But what specific behavioral characteristics and traits make up these important ingredients?

The nine behavioral skills are:

1. Eye Communication

2. Posture and Movement

3. Gestures and Facial Expressions

4. Voice and Vocal Variety

5. Dress and Appearance

6. Language, Nonwords, and Pauses

7. Listener Involvement

8. Humor

9. The Natural Self

Hundreds of stimuli go into each behavioral skill area. These are subtle refinements in the listener's perception. But of these hundreds, there are only about half a dozen key elements for each of the nine skill areas. Improving your interpersonal communication skills comes from making these key elements into behaviors you practice habitually.

In this part of the book, we first look at habits and how we can work to replace less effective habits with those that will help improve our interpersonal communications. The remaining four parts then break down the nine behavioral skills into categories, evaluating and working to improve each skill as it relates to the categories of:

Developing Connection (Part 2)

Developing Energy (Part 3)

Developing Credibility (Part 4)

Interacting with Your Audience (Part 5)

Understanding Habitual Behaviors

All behaviors come from habits, and all of us have hundreds of interpersonal communication habits. Some of these are positive but some of them are negative. And all habits can be changed.

OBSERVING HABITS

Think about the following habits you have. Those described below are harmless but ingrained:

		Y	N
1.	Fold your arms. Now do it the opposite way. Notice that, when you fold your arms, you automatically had one way to do it. When you tried the opposite way, did it seem strange and uncomfortable?	❏	❏
2.	Clasp your hands together, putting one thumb over the other. Now reverse the process. Was one way more comfortable for you?	❏	❏
3.	Do you always brush your teeth in the morning or at night?	❏	❏
4.	Do you have the same order when you wash your hands or face or take a shower?	❏	❏
5.	Do you always take the same route to work, or do you vary the route?	❏	❏

None of these habits are necessarily good or bad, but they are habits. And because they're habits, *you seem to have no choice about how you do them at the conscious level*.

The point isn't to analyze which way you fold your arms or how you wash your hands. These things aren't important, so it doesn't make much sense to change these habits. But there's value in identifying how ingrained we are in habitual behavior. When it comes to improving how we communicate, there *are* habits that are worth changing! In interpersonal communications, some habits either enhance or detract from your effectiveness. These are the ones we are targeting in this book.

Changing Your Habits

To change any habit takes practice—framing, forming, and molding the mind to do certain physical behaviors that are repeated over and over. In his book *Psycho-Cybernetics,* Maxwell Maltz wrote that it takes 21 days to change a habit. Other studies have verified this.

The problem is that habits can seem like an incessant monkey on our backs. The only way to get rid of the monkey is methodically, step by step. It's the same with our habits. To change them requires awareness, willingness, and work – practice!

PRACTICING THE PROCESS OF CHANGING HABITS

To sensitize yourself to your habits and increase your habit-changing skills, start small and practice by completing this exercise:

1. Identify one simple, small everyday habit you'd like to change. For example: Dedicating 30 minutes per day that you normally spend in social networking applications (such as Twitter and Facebook) and replacing it with 30 minutes reading a book you want to read.

   _____

   _____

2. Now identify three habits you' have throughout the day that you'd like to change. For example: In the morning, you may normally have two cups of coffee, so commit to changing that habit to just one cup. In the afternoon, you may skip lunch, so commit to planning ahead to make sure you eat something at lunch. In the evening, you may come home and unwind watching television, so commit to dedicating twenty minutes exercising or reading before watching television.

   _____

   _____

   _____

As creatures of habit, we don't easily change, so don't give up if you can't change your habits overnight. Spend 21 days dedicated to changing these habits and see if you don't get results!

Four Stages of Learning

Maslow provides a valuable conceptual framework to understand how we learn anything. As we work through the stages, we advance from a lack of awareness of what we don't know to knowing something so well that we don't even have to think about it.

Stage 1: Unconscious Incompetence—
We don't know that we don't know.

An energetic two-year-old boy wants to ride a bike that he sees his older brother riding. But he doesn't know that he doesn't know how to ride it. All he says is, "Mommy, I want to ride the bike." Most of us in business who've never had extensive feedback about our interpersonal skills are at this state of unconscious incompetence. We simply aren't aware of our interpersonal communication habits.

Stage 2: Conscious Incompetence—
We know that we don't know.

At this stage, we learn that we aren't competent at something. This often comes as a rude awakening. The two-year-old boy gets on a bike and falls off. He has immediately gone from stage one to stage two and knows that he doesn't know how to ride a bike. The same thing happens with a communicator when he finds out for the first time that he has a distracting habit, such as the "slow blink" or the "fig leaf" gesture.

Stage 3: Conscious Competence—
We work at what we don't know.

Here, we consciously make an effort to learn a new skill. Practice, drill, and repetition are at the forefront. This is where most learning takes place. It takes effort and work. The little boy carefully steers and balances and pedals and thinks of what he's doing, step by step. The person with a slow blink (or a fig leaf or other distracting habit) consciously works at changing the habit.

Stage 4: Unconscious Competence—
We don't have to think about knowing it.

Here, the skill takes over automatically at an unconscious level. The little boy rides his bike without even thinking about it. He can whistle, talk, sing, or engage his mind in other things at the same time. A speaker with a distracting habit who has learned to overcome it through practice doesn't have to concentrate on not doing the distracting habit.

Four Stages of Speaking

The four stages of speaking are related to the four stages of learning, although they aren't parallel. All communicators are in one of the four stages of speaking. To advance from one to the next requires going through the four stages of learning.

Stage 1: The Nonspeaker

People at this level avoid public speaking at all costs. Their mind-set is one of terror. These people go to great lengths to avoid speaking formally. They sometimes get trapped but, in general, are adept at finding excuses (like illness) so they won't have to present themselves or their ideas publicly. Their interpersonal communication skills tend to be low, and they generally work in jobs that don't require speaking skills.

Stage 2: The Occasional Speaker

People at this level reluctantly accept speaking assignments. They almost never volunteer. They recognize, however, that they must be able to present their ideas if they want to get ahead. They speak when necessary. Their fear is inhibiting, but not debilitating. This is the easiest stage to advance from—just by practicing the act of speaking.

Stage 3: The Willing Speaker

Fear isn't a drawback at this level. The mindset is one of tension. These speakers have learned to use emotions positively. They speak their mind in business meetings. In general, they're willing to put themselves out front—although they sometimes need a little nudge—and they know they do well. But they still have some trepidation.

Stage 4: The Leader

Speaking stimulates these folks. They're driven to present themselves and their ideas—they know the rewards to be reaped. Leaders speak for a living by motivating people and speaking up and out in all situations. They can inspire, and their roles in business are, by definition, as leaders.

Video Feedback Changes Personal Perceptions

As seen in the four stages of learning, awareness of habits is critical to any behavior change. Feedback enables this awareness, which is why feedback is so important to creating change. In interpersonal communications, video feedback is especially effective.

Our effectiveness in interpersonal communications is directly related to our confidence level. It's valuable, therefore, to use video feedback for an objective look at how we come across to others. People often find out they're better than they thought they were.

CASE STUDY: San Francisco State University Video Feedback

San Francisco State University sponsored a study documenting such changes in perception.[2] A statistically valid survey was done with 2,000 participants in an intensive two-day video feedback program. They placed themselves in four stages of speaking *before* having video feedback and then again *after* seeing themselves in different communicating circumstances during the two-day period. Following are the results:

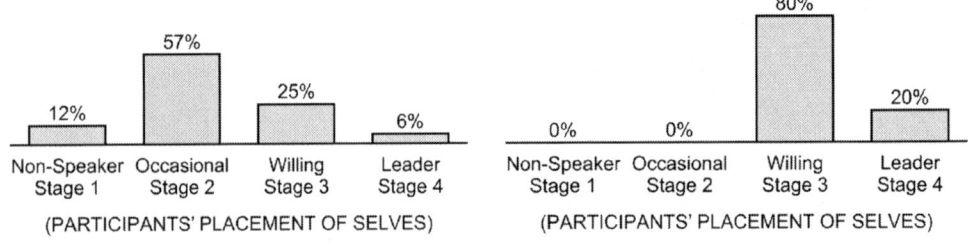

BEFORE VIDEO FEEDBACK PROGRAM

Non-Speaker Stage 1	Occasional Stage 2	Willing Stage 3	Leader Stage 4
12%	57%	25%	6%

(PARTICIPANTS' PLACEMENT OF SELVES)

AFTER VIDEO FEEDBACK PROGRAM

Non-Speaker Stage 1	Occasional Stage 2	Willing Stage 3	Leader Stage 4
0%	0%	80%	20%

(PARTICIPANTS' PLACEMENT OF SELVES)

After viewing themselves on video, participants realized their speaking ability was better than they thought. This elevated their perceptions of themselves and reduced their trepidation in speaking up in the future.

---

[2] San Francisco State University College of Business Study, 1985

Video Feedback – Record Yourself

As the San Francisco State University study reveals, observing yourself on video is valuable insight into how others perceive you when you communicate, most often revealing a dramatic difference in how you perceive yourself. The ability to see yourself is a powerful tool in improving your confidence as well as in identifying areas of improvement. One of the best ways you can hone in on both your strengths and your weaknesses in interpersonal communication is to capture yourself on video in a multitude of speaking environments: meetings, presentations, informal one-on-one communications – any and every setting in which you're communicating face-to-face with other people.

Tip: Record Yourself with Flip Video.

Any video recording device can be used to record yourself, but I recommend using equipment that's quick and easy to use on the fly, such as Flip Video cameras. Remember the goal of self-recording is to capture yourself communicating in as many settings as possible; this requires fast and flexible tools, ready to record on a moment's notice.

Flip Video

Compact, affordable, easy to use, High-Definition DVD camcorder made by Pure Digital Technologies (www.theflip.com).

Part Summary

In this part, you learned how to use the keys to **effective interpersonal communication**. You learned that **verbal**, **vocal**, and **visual cues** are the keys to believability. You learned that the **first brain** and the **new brain** process information differently and often unconciously direct our thinking. Finally, you learned that there are **nine behavioral skills** that are the primary ingredients of high-level interpersonal communications.

P A R T 2

Developing Connection

" *People have a hunger to connect with other people. They're desperate to know that you're not lying to them or misleading them.*"

– Augusten Burroughs

In this part:

Eye Contact Saved His Life

He began by telling about being a soldier in Vietnam. One evening, he and his buddies were pinned down in a bunker. His fellow soldiers were killed, and he was hit three times—once each in his right shoulder, his right thigh, and his left side.

Lying on the ground, he thought that any moment he'd die. He visualized his heart pumping all the blood out of his left side… and then just quitting… and he'd be dead.

About that time the Vietcong soldiers came up and started going through the dead American soldiers' bodies, taking their valuables—watches, rings, money, even knocking gold fillings out of their teeth.

One of the soldiers came up to him, reached down for his watch, and discovered he was still alive when the young man jerked his hand away. Immediately, the enemy soldier pointed his gun between the young man's eyes. The young man knew he was about to die.

He told how he looked up into the soldier's eyes, with as much feeling and emotion as he could muster, shook his head from side to side, and said, "No… no… please don't kill me!"

After a moment the enemy soldier could no longer handle it emotionally, broke eye contact, and pulled his gun away. Just then another Vietcong soldier yelled something. The young man assumed he asked if he was still alive, because the soldier yelled something back, which he assumed was "Yes." Then the other soldier yelled again. My friend assumed he yelled, "Kill him!" because once again the soldier pointed his gun at him and was about to pull the trigger.

Again, the young man looked deeply into his enemy's eyes, nodded his head from side to side, and said, "No… no… please don't kill me… please don't."

After an incredibly painful pause, even though he couldn't understand the language, the Vietcong soldier once again backed down, broke eye contact, pulled his gun away, pointed it into the ground a few feet away, and pulled the trigger. He then yelled something to the other soldier and walked away.

From *Integrity Selling* by Ron Willingham

Developing Connection

As demonstrated in the story of the soldiers, eye communication can make the difference between life and death. In business and personal communications, eye communication is critical for connecting with your listener – so important that this entire chapter is devoted to the behavioral skill of eye communication.

Communication without connection is futile. In both one-on-one situations and with large groups, eye communication is the catalyst to connecting with your audience.

Eye communication is the most important skill in your personal impact toolbox. It literally connects mind to mind, since your eyes are the only part of your central nervous system that directly connects with another person. When your eyes meet the eyes of another person, you make a First Brain-to-First Brain connection. When you fail to make that connection, it matters very little what you say.

Eye Communication

> *An eye can threaten like a loaded and leveled gun; or can insult like hissing and kicking; or in its altered mood, by beams of kindness, make the heart dance with joy.*"
>
> **–Ralph Waldo Emerson**

Eye communication makes or breaks the effectiveness of your interpersonal communications. No other behavioral skill can develop or destroy connection, trust, and believability more than what your eyes communicate.

Benefits of Good Eye Communication

In addition to connecting you with your audience, good eye communication provides many benefits to you—the speaker—as you communicate.

Good eye communication:

> ▶ Reduces your nervousness

> ▶ Increases your confidence

> ▶ Focuses your thoughts

> ▶ Motivates your movement

> ▶ Hones your ability to read your audience

Behavioral Objective

The objective of effective eye communication is to connect with your listener. To do this, we must understand the desirable and undesirable dynamics of how and what eye contact communicates. Simply making eye contact isn't enough. Good eye communication means more than just a fleeting glance.

Your goal in developing your eye communication skills is to *look sincerely and steadily at another person.*

In individual communications, normal eye communication should be from five to 15 seconds. To individuals in a group, it should be four to five seconds. Make this a habit, so that when you're under pressure, you maintain a confident eye pattern, without the need to think about it.

Keys to Effective Eye Communication

Awareness is the foundation of effective eye communication. Consider these tendencies and how they apply to your own inclinations in eye communication.

▶ **Five Seconds for More Effectiveness**

The "three I's" of eye communication are intimacy, intimidation, and involvement. Intimacy and intimidation mean looking at another person for a long period—from ten seconds to a minute or more. But more than 90% of our personal communications (especially in business settings) call for *involvement.* When we talk to others and are excited, enthusiastic, and confident, we usually look at them for five to 10 seconds before looking away. This is natural in one-on-one communication. It's also what you should strive for in all situations—whether speaking to one person or to a thousand. This five-second period is what listeners are comfortable with in the majority of their communications.

▶ **Beware of the "Eye Dart"**

What most of us tend to do when we feel pressure is to glance at anything but our listener. Our eyes tend to dart every which way like those of a scared rabbit. This conveys nervousness, which undermines our credibility. Anything other than looking directly at your listener increases the tendency toward darting eyes and makes our listener uncomfortable.

▶ **Beware of the "Slow Blink"**

As disconcerting as the "eye dart" is the "slow blink," in which you might keep your eyelids closed for up to two or three seconds. It conveys the message, "I really don't want to be here." Usually, your listeners won't want to be either.

▶ **Speaking to Large Groups**

When addressing a large group, extended eye communication (five seconds) is particularly important. In a large group, audience members in close proximity to an individual you're actually looking at will sense that you're looking at them. The farther back the individuals, the more people will feel included in your gaze. As a result, you can "cover" many people in one five-second gaze before shifting your eye contact to another section of the group.

▶ **Eye Communication and Television**

When you're being interviewed on video or television, it's important to have good, steady eye communication with the interviewer and any others seen through the camera. Never look directly at the camera. The audience is observing you through the means of the camera, so treat the camera as the observer it really is.

Examples of Poor Eye Communication

▶ Judy Sandler is an outside salesperson for a major corporation. She has a problem with "eye dart." Even in casual conversations, her eyes flit about like those of a high-strung thoroughbred. When she talks with clients or her peers, her "eye dart" goes into high gear. Result: She comes across as shifty and untrustworthy. She fails to connect with her listeners' First Brain—and sales that could have been hers go to the competition.

▶ Marion James is a personnel director for a major corporation. When she interviews people, she rarely looks them in the eye and often gazes out the window while talking. This unconscious habit makes her appear uninterested and distant.

▶ Doug Thomas is the minister of a small church. In the pulpit, he often closes his eyes for two or three seconds while speaking. Perhaps he's unconsciously imitating the behavior of another pastor he admires, but this habit makes him appear aloof. Worse, it carries over into his personal conversations. His parishioners see him as cold and detached—the exact opposite of the way Doug sees himself.

▶ Kathy is the manager of an IT department. When she talks to people, she tends to keep her eyes closed two to three seconds between glances, causing perhaps a calm stance, but giving the impression of aloofness, shyness, or some other form of not caring. This habit pattern also carries into her formal presentations. She doesn't know she has "slow blink," which causes her listeners to feel distance.

▶ John is a film producer who habitually looks at the lower right cheek of his listeners. He gives an impression of awkwardness and distance without knowing it.

▶ As a professional speaker, Pat excites audiences with dramatic personal stories and anecdotes—except that she undermines her personal impact by looking at people in her audience for about half a second or less. Pat believes she has good eye contact, but the individuals in her audience don't feel she's talking right to them

Do you see yourself in any of these examples? If so, there's hope. You can improve your eye communication by practicing the following suggestions and exercises.

Improving Your Eye Communication

Eye communication problems are curable. Don't
assume that making occasional, glancing eye contact
is enough. Good eye communication is more than a
glance. True eye communication involves using your
eyes to make a First Brain-to-First Brain connection.

Listed below are skill development exercises and tips to develop your eye
communication skills in the dozens of interpersonal communications you have
daily. Practice each of these every day. At first, these practices may feel awkward or
embarrassing; but as with other learned behaviors, regular practice will increase
your confidence, and your eye communication will show steady improvement.

1. **Where Do You Look?**

   In your next 10 conversations, determine where you generally look when
   you talk to others. Note that you don't look directly into both eyes. You may
   look either at a person's left eye or right eye, but it's impossible to look at
   both at the same time. In one-on-one conversations, our eyes tend to move
   around the face, but there's one primary place most of us tend to rest. Find
   where your spot is—right eye? bridge of the nose? left eye? directly
   between the eyes? Any resting place near the eyes is acceptable. Not
   acceptable is anywhere else (the floor, over your listener's shoulder, etc.).

   Once you've found your pattern, increase your awareness and sensitize
   yourself to the complexities of eye communication. Then try to look
   somewhere else and feel the dissonance. This will help desensitize you to
   feelings of awkwardness when you might not want to look directly at
   someone but should for effectiveness.

2. **Reinforce the Five-Second Habit**

   When you're in a meeting or giving a speech, ask a friend to count how
   long you look at specific individuals. Consciously keep five-second eye
   communication with those in the group with whom you're communicating.

3. **Increase Sensitivity**

   Talk to a partner for about a minute. Ask him to look away from you after
   15 seconds as you continue talking. For the rest of the exercise, have him
   look anywhere else but at you while he's still listening. How does this feel?
   Reverse the process and then discuss the relevance of eye communication in
   verbal conversations. Then notice how often good eye contact is lacking at
   certain social functions (such as parties). Practice better eye contact in these
   informal situations and realize what a difference it makes to a conversation.

4. Relieve Intimidation

If you feel uncomfortable with an individual you must talk to (such as in a job interview or a meeting with the company president), try looking at that person's forehead. To experiment with this, get in a conversation with a partner sitting four or five feet away. Look at the middle of her forehead, just above her eyes. She'll think you have good eye communication with her, but you won't feel as if you're in touch at all. This helps reduce the emotional connection, so it's almost like talking to a wall. Reverse the process, so your partner can experience the same phenomenon.

5. Analyze Eye Communication in Yourself and Others

Observe others and notice how different an individual's eye communication patterns make you feel about the person. Ask friends how they feel about your eye communication. Ask a friend or associate to analyze your eye contact in various communication circumstances.

6. Get Video Feedback

Nothing reveals your eye communication skills clearer than video footage of yourself communicating. Record yourself at every opportunity, in a variety of communicating situations. You'll quickly become aware of your eye movements—both length of eye contact and idiosyncrasies such as the "eye dart" or "slow blink." In addition to recording yourself or having a friend record you while you're practicing or actually giving a presentation, you can also fine-tune your skills in a training course providing extensive video feedback, such as Decker Communications. (www.decker.com)

7. Watch News Programs on Television or Online

You'll increase your awareness and "eye savvy" by seeing real people in pressure situations. Such opportunities are in abundance on news programs. Observe people being themselves, attempting to persuade while under pressure. Note their eye communication patterns. Specialized news programs offering in-depth exploration into a particular current event (such as Dateline NBC, 60 Minutes, and 20/20) provide excellent opportunities to observe people when they are put on the defensive and the heat is on. The First Brain reveals itself in eye communication. Notice telltale signs of fear, anger, arrogance, evasion, or sadness in the eyes. Look for signs of confidence and believability. See how eye communication can enhance or betray a person's credibility and likeability.

8. Practice One-on-One

At every opportunity, ask a friend to assist you in increasing your awareness of your eye communication patterns. Ask your friend to keep track of your eye patterns and length of movements during a normal conversation. Have your friend silently count while you make eye contact, and record it so that he or she can tell you later. Then, get an average count on how long you tend to look at a person. Work on pushing that average to five seconds or more.

9. Practice with a Paper Audience

Practice with a paper audience when preparing for a presentation. Draw faces on Post-it notes and arrange them on chairs or on the wall to mimic your actual audience, making sure to place Post-it faces on the fringes (edges and corners) of your audience. Then give your presentation to your paper audience, paying close attention to dedicating at least 5 seconds of eye contact to each face, including the faces at the fringes.

"Can I listen without making eye contact?"

Eye Communication Patterns in Business

You use your eyes to communicate 90% of the time in business (excluding the telephone). As you communicate with colleagues, customers, managers, and other business associates, concentrate on how you look at them. Envision how you look when you're upset or pleased. As a salesperson, focus on how you look at tough clients before a sale. Compare that to how you look when you've just closed a sale.

Notice the eye patterns of others during job interviews and performance appraisals. Then take your newfound awareness and apply it to more effective and confident eye patterns of your own.

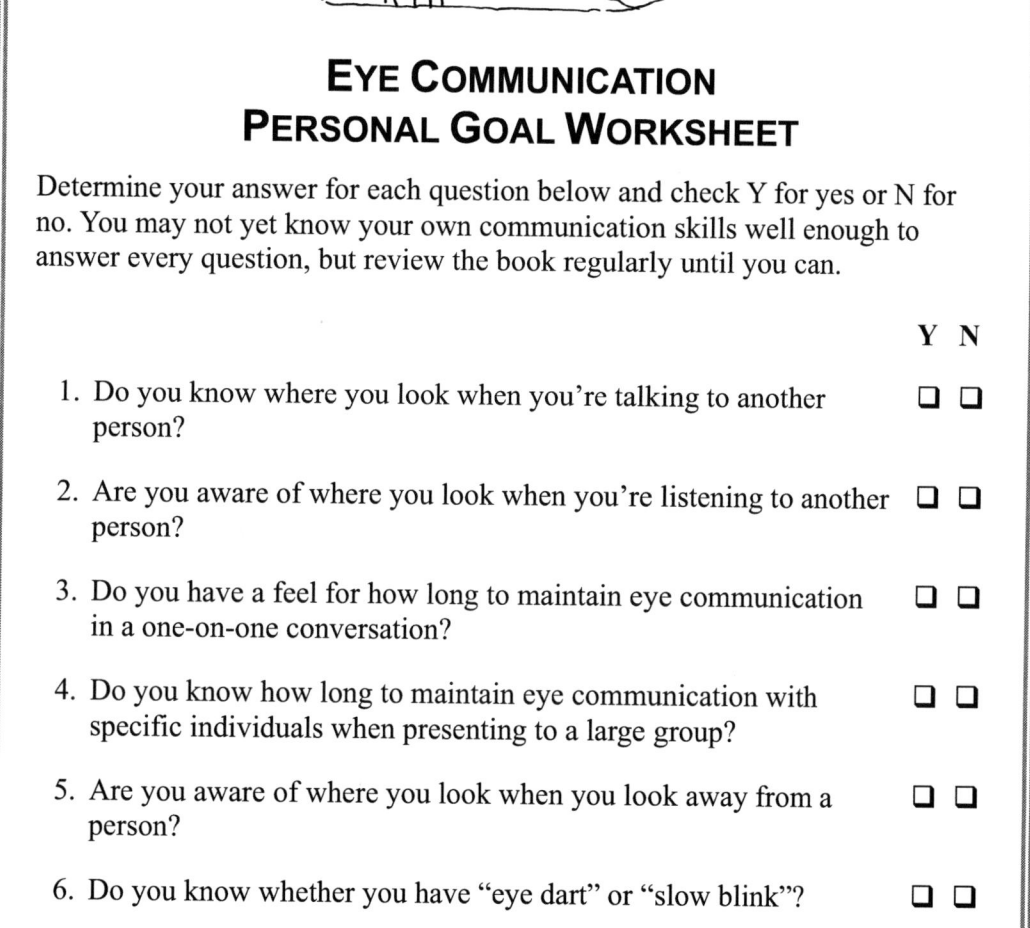

EYE COMMUNICATION PERSONAL GOAL WORKSHEET

Determine your answer for each question below and check Y for yes or N for no. You may not yet know your own communication skills well enough to answer every question, but review the book regularly until you can.

	Y	N
1. Do you know where you look when you're talking to another person?	❑	❑
2. Are you aware of where you look when you're listening to another person?	❑	❑
3. Do you have a feel for how long to maintain eye communication in a one-on-one conversation?	❑	❑
4. Do you know how long to maintain eye communication with specific individuals when presenting to a large group?	❑	❑
5. Are you aware of where you look when you look away from a person?	❑	❑
6. Do you know whether you have "eye dart" or "slow blink"?	❑	❑
7. Do you realize that eye communication is the most important behavioral skill in interpersonal communications?	❑	❑

CONTINUED

List three habitual patterns in your eye communication that you want to modify, strengthen, or eliminate:

1. _____

   _____

   _____

   _____

2. _____

   _____

   _____

   _____

3. _____

   _____

   _____

   _____

Remember: Practice Makes Permanent

Part Summary

In this part, you learned how to **develop connection**. You learned how to use **eye communication** to look sincerely and steadily to connect with your listener. Then, you learned how to use eye communication **patterns** in business.

Developing

Energy

"The world belongs to the energetic."

–Ralph Waldo Emerson

In this part:

▶ Developing Energy

▶ Posture and Movement

▶ Gestures and Facial Expressions

▶ Voice and Vocal Variety

Developing Energy

In the same way that targeting the behavioral skill of eye communication develops our **connection** in interpersonal communication, we can chart the path of developing **energy** when we communicate. In this chapter, we target the behavioral skills of:

▶ Posture and movement

▶ Gestures and facial expressions

▶ Voice and vocal variety

By honing these behavioral skills, you'll learn how to cultivate and convey energy in all of your communications, whether speaking to one or one thousand.

Posture and Movement

> " *Stand tall. The difference between towering and cowering is totally a matter of inner posture. It's got nothing to do with height, it costs nothing, and it's more fun."*

–Malcolm Forbes

Think of a public figure you often see on TV—a newscaster, politician, celebrity, pundit. Can you think of any who are "slumpers"? Probably not many, since confidence is usually expressed through excellent posture.

How you hold yourself physically can reflect how you hold yourself psychologically. And how you hold yourself is usually how others regard you. People tend to treat you as you "ask" to be treated.

Behavioral Objective

Your goal in developing your posture and movement skills is to *stand tall and move naturally and easily.*

You must correct the general tendency to slump in both upper and lower body posture. When communicating, it's more effective to be fluid rather than locked into rigid positions. This applies to all gestures, but particularly to leg and foot movements.

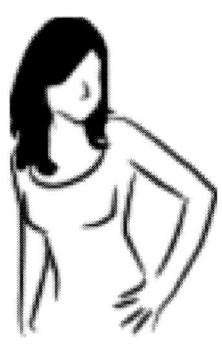

Keys to Effective Posture and Movement

There's no absolute right or wrong way to stand or move. But there are concepts that work, as described below. Be sure to adapt posture and movement concepts to your personal style.

▶ **Stand Tall**

Poor upper body posture often reflects low self-esteem. At least this is how other people see it, until they have enough information to change this opinion. Upper body posture often comes from an outdated habit pattern. Many tall people walk around hunched over, because they grew fast as adolescents and didn't want to stand out. Others simply never considered posture to be important and allowed the slouching and slumping teenage period to extend into adulthood.

▶ **Watch Your Lower Body**

A part of posture that is often neglected is the lower body. When you speak, you may decrease your effectiveness because of the way you stand. You can divert communication energy away from listeners through inappropriate body language. One common adverse posture pattern is going back on one hip. When you do this you subconsciously say, "I don't want to be here." You literally distance yourself from others. Other variations are rocking from side to side, going back and forth on heels and toes, or pacing.

▶ **Use the "Ready" Position**

To combat these negative habits, take the "ready" position, or weight forward. When you're speaking—when you're confident and want to get a message across—you have your energy forward. The ready position is leaning slightly forward so you could bounce up and down on the balls of your feet, with knees slightly flexed. It's similar to bracing for athletic competition, in which you're ready to move in any direction. With your weight forward, it's impossible to go back on one hip or rock back and forth on your heels. Get in the habit of the ready position in both formal and informal communication situations, and you'll be ready when the heat is on.

▶ **Move**

Communication and energy can't be separated. Use all of your natural energy in a positive way. When you speak, move around. In a formal setting, come out from behind the podium. This removes a barrier between you and others. In group meetings, you have room to move a bit—your feet as well as hands or arms. If seated, consider standing when you're "on" or leaning forward to give yourself more impact. Movement increases your energy, reflects confidence, and adds variety to your communications. Don't overdo it, but do move within your own natural energy level. Although high-energy people have an advantage, greater personal impact is available to all who stay conscious of using what they have.

Improving Your Posture and Movement

Listed below are several skill development exercises and tips for posture and movement to try in the dozens of interpersonal communications you have daily.

1. **See Yourself**

   You can readily monitor your posture and movement through mirrors or others' observations. Better yet, if you can arrange it, videotape yourself walking and talking, and then observe the video. Notice your upper body position—standing tall? hunching down? somewhere in between? If you cross your legs and lean against walls when you're standing informally, you'll notice that it often appears sloppy rather than casual. Try variations of the ready position to see how that looks.

2. **Walk Away from the Wall**

   Practice standing tall by aligning your body against a wall. Stand with your back and heels touching the wall. (Body structures vary, so the actual distance between your back, heels and the wall will vary between zero and a few inches.) In this position, make sure your buttocks, shoulder blades, and the back of your head are aligned with the wall (touching the wall or as close to touching the wall as possible). Your face should look straight ahead, not up or down. Hold this position for a moment or two, then slowly walk away from the wall. Shake loose a bit so you don't feel too rigid, but focus on holding the wall posture as you walk. Notice how you feel tall and project more confidence as you stand and walk with this posture. As you practice this regularly, your posture will dramatically improve.

3. **Do the "Two-Step"**

   The next time you are talking to a group, have someone count the number of steps you take (if you move at all). Often we take tentative half-steps because we want to move but feel inhibited. That degree of movement is better than none, but it still reflects exactly what we feel—tentativeness. If you do the "two-step" instead, taking at least two steps toward someone, you'll force yourself to move with apparent purpose. When you combine that with good eye communication, you'll talk and present yourself in a confident, direct fashion.

4. **Stand at Meetings**

   Experiment with posture and movement. At your next meeting, stand when you have something important to say. This gives your message more emphasis. When you go into a one-on-one meeting to sell a product or an idea, consider making a stand-up presentation, perhaps even using a visual aid, such as a flip chart.

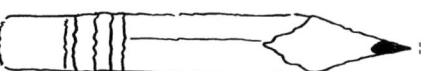

POSTURE AND MOVEMENT
PERSONAL GOALS WORKSHEET

Determine your answer to each question below and check Y for yes or N for no. You may not yet know your own communication skills well enough to answer every question, but review the book regularly until you can.

	Y	N
1. Do you lean back on one hip when speaking in a small group?	❑	❑
2. Do you cross your legs when you're standing and chatting informally?	❑	❑
3. Is your upper body posture erect—shoulders in a straight line rather than curving inward toward your chest?	❑	❑
4. When you speak formally, do you plant yourself behind a lectern or table?	❑	❑
5. Do you communicate impatience by tapping your foot or a pencil when you're listening?	❑	❑
6. Do you know if you have the "fig leaf" pose or other nervous or inhibiting gestures when addressing a group?	❑	❑
7. Do you move around when talking informally?	❑	❑

Gestures and Facial Expressions

> **We don't 'know' our presidents. We imagine them. We watch them intermittently and from afar, inferring from only a relatively few gestures and reactions what kind of people they are and whether they should be in charge. Much depends on our intuition and their ability at a handful of opportune moments to project qualities we admire and respect."**
>
> **–Meg Greenfield**

Leaders are judged by how they communicate, from prominent posture and movement to the subtlest gestures and facial expressions. Words—however eloquent and well-crafted—can't transcend the subconscious message portrayed in body language. Incongruent gestures and facial expressions can sabotage not only the energy we believe we're conveying in our communications, but also the connection and credibility we seek to establish. For this reason, bringing this behavioral skill into formation with the other behavioral skills is critical to successful communication.

To communicate effectively, we must become aware of what our gestures and facial expressions communicate to others, and we must train ourselves to align our body language with the objective of our communication.

Behavioral Objective

Your goal in developing your skills with gestures and facial expressions is *to be relaxed and natural when you speak.*

To be effective at interpersonal communication, you should have your hands and arms relaxed and natural at your sides when you're at rest. You should gesture naturally when animated and enthusiastic. You should learn to smile under pressure, in the same way you would with a natural smile when you're comfortable.

Keys to Effective Gestures and Facial Expressions

To communicate effectively, you need to be as open as possible in your face and gestures—*in a way that's natural for you*. You can work to ensure better gestures and facial expressions in the following ways:

▶ **Find Out Your Habits**

Find out how you look to others when you're under pressure. Get this to the conscious level. You can make this discovery through feedback from others, but best of all, view and observe yourself on video. You have to know what you're doing that isn't natural before you can be natural. You need to be able to recognize your habits at the level of conscious incompetence.

▶ **Find Your Nervous Gestures**

We all have gestures we tend to use when we're speaking without anything to hold onto. Find out what your primary gesture is and then do anything but that gesture. Don't try to gesture at certain words or phrases—it doesn't work well. Just concentrate on avoiding your nervous gesture. Your hands should fall to your sides when you aren't emphasizing an idea or point. When you do want the emphasis that comes from natural enthusiasm, it will occur naturally. But it can't occur if your hands are stuck in your pockets or locked in a nervous gesture or if your arms are crossed.

▶ **You Can't Over-exaggerate**

Very few people exaggerate gestures and facial expressions. It's almost possible to say that you can't over-exaggerate. Push yourself. Try to exaggerate your positive gestures. You'd be surprised at how normal they actually look. Don't worry about overdoing it.

▶ **Smile—Which Third Are You In?**

We all think that we smile much of the time. In reality, others observe us as having a very strong predisposition to either smiling or not smiling. Studies have shown that about one-third of people in business have naturally open and smiling faces. Another third tend to have neutral faces that can readily go from a smile to a serious and intense look. And another third have faces that are serious and intense, whether they think they're smiling or not.

Find out which third you're in. Ask others to help you. If you're in the easily smiling third, you have a distinct advantage in communications with others. People perceive you as open and friendly and are more open to your ideas. Another advantage is that you can also convey bad news more readily than others. If you're in the neutral third, easily moving from a smiling face to a serious one, you have flexibility. But if you're in the solemn third, you have to work on this area of your communications. You may be smiling on the inside, but your face may reflect doom and gloom on the outside. And that's exactly what you communicate. Perception is reality in the eyes of the beholder.

▶ **Remember the Personality Factor**

Your gestures, particularly your facial expressions, tend to show you to be either open and connected or closed and distant to those with whom you're communicating. Remember that people buy your ideas and are persuaded much more readily if they like you. People like people who are more open. It pays to cultivate the personality factor. Serious people, such as technocrats, analysts, programmers, engineers, and academicians, can be effective in person, but they're usually more effective in writing. Interpersonal communication means connecting with another person on an *emotional* level, not just on an intellectual level.

▶ **Smiles Have Muscles**

There's nothing mysterious about a smile, except the effect it has. It's physically caused by muscles, and they can be exercised. Practicing smiling isn't as much about moving your lips into a smile as it is about raising your cheekbones. Consider the upper part of your cheeks as apples and just lift your apples to smile. Put muscle into your smile.

▶ **Caution: Phony Smiles Don't Work**

Smiling is such an important interpersonal skill because it immediately communicates how you're feeling—or at least people perceive how you're feeling by the look on your face. So it's important to become aware of how you smile. But beware that phony smiles don't work. Not only do they not last, but they're perceived as phony. You want to train yourself to smile through practice with your facial muscles, but remember that a true smile comes from within. It's like practicing a sport and training your muscles so they're ready to use at the right time—when you're motivated by the adrenaline of competition.

Improving Your Gestures and Facial Expressions

Listed below are several skill development exercises and tips to enhance your gestures and facial expressions in the dozens of interpersonal communications you have daily.

1. **Practice Gesturing with a Partner/Observer**

   Stand six to eight feet from another person who'll be your observer. Talk about how your hands and arms feel as they're resting at your sides. Then continue talking about gestures in general and how they feel when they're natural. Gesture normally as you speak. Then exaggerate your gestures, even moving a little bit, if you feel like it, and describe to your partner how you're feeling as you do so. Make sure your gestures are exaggerated—and that they go above your waist and out to the side. Then ask your partner for feedback. She'll probably tell you that she didn't feel that you exaggerated as much as you felt you did. Reverse the process and let your partner do the gesturing and you give the feedback. Practice this exercise several times until you get a good feel for how energetic you can be without being perceived as exaggerated.

2. **Count Your Nervous Gestures**

   The next time you speak in front of a group, have someone count the number of times you display your nervous gesture. This can be at a meeting or in a formal or informal speaking situation. If your nervous gesture is the fig leaf, for example, tell this to your observer and then have him count the number of times during the presentation that you display the fig leaf. This exercise will sensitize you to how serious your problem is and serve as a starting point for modifying your behavior to do anything other than your nervous gesture.

3. **Role-Playing**

   Look at a video or TV performance of a confident, forceful, energetic speaker. You might select a leader from politics, business, or athletics as your role model. Work through the following steps as you try to emulate that person:

   ▷ Take an actual presentation, preferably a business presentation, and deliver it to an individual or group in your usual manner. (This exercise is very effective in groups.)

   ▷ Then think about how your role model might deliver it.

   ▷ Put all of yourself into acting as if you were that person delivering your material. Remember, this is just a role-play and practice, so let it all hang out.

   ▷ Then ask for feedback from the group. (If possible, videotape both presentations so you'll be able to see the difference in yourself.)

4. Watch Television with No Sound

Whether situation comedies, talk shows, or newscasts—take a look at television with the sound turned off. If you do this just five or ten minutes a day, you'll be amazed at how much is communicated by those you observe. Their interpersonal communications, believability, confidence, and credibility are largely conveyed through their gestures and facial expressions.

5. Test Your Smile

You can do this exercise alone, if you have access to a video camera. Start recording, look directly at the camera, and give a big phony smile. Describe to the camera how it feels to give that big phony smile. Spend 20 or 30 seconds with that big phony smile. Then, with the video camera continuing to record, wipe your face clean and convey what, to you, feels like a normal, easy, friendly smile. Describe how that feels on your face for 20 to 30 seconds. Then view your video footage.

If you're in the one-third of non-smilers, you may see that your phony smile doesn't look as bad as you thought, and at least it conveys some degree of openness and friendliness. At the same time, you may see that the natural smile you felt on the inside didn't show at all on the outside. Often when you think you're smiling, you're actually looking serious.

GESTURES AND FACIAL EXPRESSIONS
PERSONAL GOALS WORKSHEET

Determine your answer to each question below and check Y for yes or N for no. You may not yet know your own communication skills well enough to answer every question, but review the book regularly until you can.

	Y	N
1. Do you smile under pressure or become stone-faced?	❑	❑
2. When you talk on the phone, do you find yourself smiling rather than frowning?	❑	❑
3. Do you have an inhibiting gesture—an awkward place where your hands tend to go when speaking under pressure?	❑	❑
4. Do you ever raise your hand or arm above waist level when making a presentation to a group?	❑	❑
5. Do you lean forward and gesture when you're seated, just as you do when you're making a presentation?	❑	❑
6. Do you communicate impatience by drumming your fingers on the table when you're listening?	❑	❑
7. Do your fingers twitch if you try to keep them at your sides when you're speaking to a group?	❑	❑

Voice and Vocal Variety

> ❝ *The devil hath not, in all his quiver's choice, an arrow for the heart like a sweet voice.* ❞

–Byron

Your voice is the primary vehicle to carry your message. It's like transportation—you can have an old jalopy that rattles along or a smooth-running, finely tuned automobile. Both get you to your destination, but the quality of the ride can vary greatly.

Behavioral Objective

Your goal in developing your voice and vocal variety is to *use your voice as a rich, resonant instrument*, whether you're communicating with others in person, on the phone, or in a group setting. You want to command people's attention and not allow your voice to be a barrier to action.

"Hard figures are not available, but Henry's poem explores the essence of our situation."

Keys to Effective Voice and Vocal Variety

The keys in this section are among the most important tools for making a positive impression with your voice, whether you're speaking to one person or a thousand.

▶ **Your Voice Transmits Energy**

The excitement and enthusiasm you feel should be directly conveyed by the sound of your voice. We quickly fall into vocal habit patterns that are difficult to change. But they can be changed or relearned. Record your voice to become aware of how much energy, or how little, you transmit to others.

▶ **Your Vocal Tone and Quality Can Count for 84% of Your Message**

UCLA Professor Mehrabian's research shows that your vocal tone— intonation, resonance, and delivery—accounts for 84% of the believability you have *when people can't see you*—such as when you talk on the phone.

▶ **The Sounds of One Word**

Subtleties of voice are far greater than we think. We can read an enormous amount into the vocal tone of people on the phone during the first few seconds. Call someone you know well and listen as they say, "hello." You can almost tell their mood by that single word.

▶ **The Four Aspects of Voice**

The four components that make up your vocal expression are relaxation, breathing, projection, and resonance. Each can be altered through exercises to expand your vocal effectiveness. All work together to give your voice its unique characteristics.

▶ **Use Vocal Variety**

Vocal variety is a great way to keep people interested and involved. Use a "roller coaster"—consciously lift your voice and then let it plummet. This will make you aware of a monotone and get you in the habit of putting variety into your voice.

▶ **Don't Read Speeches**

One of the greatest culprits of a monotone delivery in public speaking is reading the speech aloud. Writing, reading, and speaking are different communication media. When you speak, simply use notes and outlines of main ideas. Then your mind has to select words spontaneously. This forces your voice to be active, animated, and natural as you continually think, adapt, and alter your content.

Improving Your Voice and Vocal Variety

The following skill development exercises and tips can enhance your voice and vocal variety in the dozens of interpersonal communications you have daily.

1. **Emphasize the Right Word**

   Read the sentence, "Now is the time for change," six times, emphasizing a different word each time. Notice the difference in the meaning each time. Emphasis is critical. Experiment with emphasizing the appropriate word in your everyday conversations.

2. **The Voice of the Company**

   Call five companies at random from the phone book and listen to how they answer the phone. Rate them by the vocal tone and quality. How does your organization rate on initial image? And how do you *personally* rate when you answer your phone?

3. **Good and Bad Voices**

   List five people you know or hear on radio or television with attractive, pleasant vocal deliveries. List five people who have poor vocal deliveries. Analyze why they're good or bad.

4. **Record Yourself**

   The best exercise to develop your vocal skills is to record yourself. Do this as often as possible. Record a phone conversation, a business meeting, and even a casual conversation with a friend. The most important improvement mechanism for your vocal delivery is audio feedback.

EXERCISE YOUR VOICE

For each of the following exercises, stand, leaning forward in the ready position, and maintain a deep, easy breathing pattern throughout.

A. Breathe from the Diaphragm

1. Place your hands on your lower rib cage.

2. Inhale deeply through your nose. The expansion you feel in your lower rib cage is caused by your diaphragm muscle expanding and dropping as the air pushes against it. Your shoulders shouldn't move.

3. Exhale, allowing the air to escape slowly through your slightly open mouth. You'll feel a depression around your lower rib cage as the diaphragm rises like a trampoline to support and propel the air.

4. Repeat Steps 1 to 3 several times until you find the rhythm in which your breathing is effortless. You should have the sensation of being calm yet full of energy.

5. Do the exercise one more time, moving one hand from the side of your lower rib cage. When you inhale, your breath should push your hand away from the abdominal area. If this doesn't happen, you aren't breathing deeply enough for the diaphragm to do its job.

Remember: While inhaling, the abdominal area should fill up first and more fully than your chest.

B. Add Sound to Your Breathing Exercise

1. Repeat the instructions from the previous exercise, but when you exhale, do it as you say "ah."

2. Relax your jaw, open your mouth, and sustain the "ah" for as long as it's strong and lively. (Don't let yourself run out of air and be sure not to put tension in your throat.)

CONTINUED

C. Tone and Relax Your Head and Neck

1. Relax your jaw so your mouth is slightly open.

2. Slowly drop (don't push) your head to your chest—bring it back to the upright, centered position—drop it to your right shoulder, then back to center—drop it to your left shoulder, then back to center—drop it to the back, return to center.

3. Beginning at center, do two head rolls slowly to the right. Return to center and do two head rolls slowly to the left; return to center.

4. Monitor your breathing throughout; make sure you are'ot holding your breath. Keep your jaw loose.

D. Tone and Relax Your Shoulders

1. With your hands at your sides, clench your fists.

2. Lift your shoulders to your ears (or try to!).

3. Drop your shoulders and release your fists with a thrust, sighing as you exhale.

E. Tone and Relax Using Shoulder Rolls

1. Do six slow shoulder rolls to the back, keeping your jaw loose. Feel your chest expand; sigh as you exhale.

2. Do six slow shoulder rolls to the front. Sigh as you exhale.

F. Tone and Relax Your Face ("The Prune")

1. Make the "tiniest" face you can. Pucker your lips, close your eyes, and tighten your muscles.

2. Open into the "widest" face you can make.

3. Return to the tight position, and then try to move your entire face (not your head) to the right-hand side.

4. Try to move your face to the left-hand side.

5. Return to the wide position and repeat the exercise.

CONTINUED

G. Tone and Relax Your Lips ("The Motorboat")

1. Take a deep breath.

2. Pucker your lips.

3. As you exhale, force the air through your puckered lips. (This will result in a "motorboat" sound and will direct vibrating energy to your lips while relaxing them.)

H. Increase Your Resonance ("King Kong" and "Yawning")

1. Drop your jaw and allow it to hang loosely.

2. Inhale deeply through your nose, allowing your belly to fill up first and more fully than your chest.

   a. As you exhale, say "KING KONG, DING DONG, BING BONG," lowering the tone each time so that the final "BONG" gently eases down into a lower and lower range, until you reach bottom. Do this gently and avoid pushing on your throat muscles.

   b. As you exhale, relax your jaw. Open your mouth wide and allow your throat to open: Start on a high note and lower your pitch gradually until you reach bottom—as when yawning. Do this gently. Avoid pushing on your throat muscles.

I. Project Your Voice

1. Say a test sentence in a conversational tone.

2. Inhale deeply through your nose, allowing your belly to fill first and more fully than your chest.

3. Exhale while saying your test sentence, with the mental image of placing your voice 10 to 20 rows beyond the last row of an imaginary audience.

4. Monitor yourself to make sure you're letting your breath support your voice rather than pushing the sound from your throat.

J. Control and Vary Your Pitch

Say test sentences in a singsong fashion. Play with various pitches and experiment with a range of tones. Song lyrics and poems work well.

CONTINUED

K. Practice Your Pacing

Practice test sentences while varying the speed of your delivery between and within them. Insert pauses for additional variety. Record yourself to hear the difference. Read interesting newspaper articles aloud and exaggerate the pace.

All of the preceding exercises need regular practice. As when learning to ride a bicycle, repeat each exercise until it becomes a habit. Whenever possible, practice with a friend.

VOICE AND VOCAL VARIETY
PERSONAL GOALS WORKSHEET

Determine your answer to each question below and check Y for yes or N for no. You may not yet know your own communication skills well enough to answer every question, but review the book regularly until you can.

	Y	N
1. Do you project your voice to others, rather than simply speaking?	❏	❏
2. Do you know if you have a high nasal or low resonant voice, or somewhere in between?	❏	❏
3. Are you aware when your voice goes into a monotone and for what reasons?	❏	❏
4. Has anyone ever complimented you on your voice? (If so, why? If not, why not?)	❏	❏
5. Does your phone voice differ from your speaking voice?	❏	❏
6. Are you aware of what impact your voice has over the phone?	❏	❏
7. Do you know how to "put a smile" in your voice?	❏	❏
8. When you hear a person answer a phone for an organization, do you think about what image is conveyed?	❏	❏

Part Summary

In this part, you learned how to **develop energy**. You learned how to use **posture** and **movement** to stand tall and move naturally and easily. Next, you learned how to use **gestures** and **facial expressions** to be relaxed and natural when you speak. Finally, you learned how to use **voice** and **vocal variety** to use your voice as a rich, resonant instrument.

P A R T 4

Developing
Credibility

❝*What you do speaks so loud I can't hear what you say.*❞

–Ralph Waldo Emerson

In this part:

▶ Developing Credibility

▶ Dress and Appearance

▶ Language, Nonwords, and Pauses

Developing Credibility

Credibility is established as soon as we see a person. It's then enhanced or diminished as soon as soon as that person begins to speak. In this chapter, we target the behavior skills associated with dress and appearance; as well as language, nonwords, and pauses.

In his best-selling book, *Blink*, Malcolm Gladwell introduces "thin-slicing." His research confirms what Decker Communications has found in training tens of thousands of people: We make our opinions about credibility very quickly by what we see and hear. This is what Gladwell calls thin-slicing, and he uses two seconds as its benchmark . In just two seconds, police officers in critical situations must assess the facts by what they see and immediately determine whether or not to draw their weapons.

These types of instantaneous decisions are primarily governed by our First Brain. Such reactionary processing is done quickly and unconsciously. Likewise, credibility is determined by First Brain processing, on a subconscious level, in immediate response to the visual and verbal cues presented.

In order to develop credibility, we must focus on the immediate visual impression we make on our audiences (*dress and appearance*) as well as the powerful verbal impression we make (*language, nonwords and pauses*) that improves or detracts from our credibility.

Dress and Appearance

You never get a second chance to make a good first impression."

–John Molloy

You might be surprised to know the effect that your physical appearance has on people. The impact it makes on your listener is probably more significant than you realize. It isn't a superficial thing. Rather it communicates extensively to others how you feel about yourself. It also shows what you sometimes do just to get attention.

We form immediate and vivid impressions of people during the first two seconds we see them. Experts estimate that it takes another 30 seconds to add 50% more impression (negative or positive) to the impression we got in the first two seconds. If you take this concept further, you can calculate that it takes three minutes to add 50% more to the 30-second impression. First impressions are powerful.

Behavioral Objective

Your goal in developing your skills with dress and appearance is to *look appropriate for the environment you're in, as well as for yourself.*

There isn't so much a right or wrong way to dress or groom as there is an appropriate way. This means appropriate—first of all in how comfortable *you* feel. This is more important than what others feel. If you feel uncomfortable, you won't communicate very effectively. Your appearance also should be appropriate to the company you're in, considering others' expectations, your geographical setting, the time of day, social situation, circumstances, and so on.

Keys to Effective Use of Dress and Appearance

Because 90% of our body is covered by clothing, we need to be aware of what our clothes are communicating. (When we're uncovered, the same principle applies. Considering this, if we spend time at the beach or pool, we might be motivated to exercise a bit more.)

The 10% of the body not normally covered by clothes is largely the face and hair. This is the most important 10% of all because this is where people look. Others' impressions of us are the result of how we groom our head—for example, hairstyle, makeup, and jewelry for women; hairstyle, facial hair, or lack of it for men.

Most of us dress based on past habits, because we're creatures of habit. Take a careful and conscious look at how you dress and groom. Do you pick out a certain color because you always have? Does that color work for you? Do you wear certain shoes or eyeglasses because those are what you wore in college? Are they still *appropriate* today?

The following examples illustrate the importance of evaluating dress and appearance for the messages they convey.

Examples: Dress and Appearance

The following examples illustrate the importance of evaluating dress and appearance for the messages they convey.

▶ A writer for *The New Yorker*, Malcolm Gladwell became a business phenomenon with his book, *The Tipping Point*. Afterward, he decided to let his hair grow from a closely cropped style into a full afro. He found that people's reactions to him were significantly different from when he had short hair and that he was stopped on the highway by police officers more often. Why did he experience people treating him differently based on hairstyle, he wondered. These experiences led to his writing the influential book, *Blink*, which explores the power of first impressions—those made, seemingly, "in the *blink* of an eye."

▶ A film producer for many years did business mostly in the sans-necktie "uniform" of a filmmaker. When speaking to business groups, he'd concede to wearing a tie and jacket. Today, more enlightened about dress and appearance, he's embarrassed to think of his audience's reaction the time he spoke to the 50 managers of a client company—while wearing a plaid sports jacket, vivid red shirt, and black knit tie.

Do you see yourself in these examples? If so, there's hope. You can improve your dress and appearance by practicing the following suggestions and exercises.

Improving Your Dress and Appearance

Listed below are skill development exercises and tips to help you enhance your dress and appearance in the dozens of interpersonal communications you have daily.

1. **The First Two Seconds**

   When you next meet a person for the first time, consciously keep a mental picture of how you *felt* about that person after the first impression. Then analyze how much came from dress, from expression, from hairstyle, from eye contact, from jewelry, and so on. What made a positive impression and what made a distracting impression? What was neutral? Do this exercise daily. It can also be a pleasant pastime at a party or social gathering.

2. **Pick Five People**

   List the names of five people you know well. Think of how you'd *design* their dress and appearance differently. Pick it apart in detail—the clothes, shirts, skirts, ties, colors, patterns, makeup, hair, jewelry, glasses, and so on. It works best if you write out the changes so you become *consciously* aware of the differences each of these elements make.

3. **Nobody Will Tell You**

   Now that you've analyzed five other people, do the same for yourself. Analyze in detail what you do and what you should change. Realize that almost no one volunteers to tell you what needs changing. Dress and appearance is one of the most self-conscious and personally sensitive subjects in interpersonal communications, so few people tell us what they really think and feel. You can help them provide feedback by just asking. It can help verify your own analysis.

4. **Pick a New Outfit**

   Every day, look at something in a new way. Choose one area, such as your shoes, dress, suit, jacket, tie, shirt, or grooming habit. Change it. Combine it with something to give a new look. Pick an appropriate but different outfit the next time you're shopping. Dressing differently daily sensitizes you to how you feel in your dress and appearance. It also makes you more aware of how others feel about your appearance. And it will help you discover what works well.

5. See a Consultant

Because dress and appearance have a great impact on how others perceive us, it's often worth the time and expense to consult a specialist. This can be a clothes consultant, color consultant, or makeup consultant. Be sure to check referrals, because this is an area of "image intangibles" and you want to be sure you get good advice. You can consult specialized "shoppers" in department stores to assist in your clothes buying. Or seek assistance from online resources, such as www.firstimpressionmanagement.com.

6. Research, Research, Research

Read a book. John Molloy's books—*Dress for Success* in both men's and women's versions—are probably the best known. Although his opinions may not be to your taste, his research is extensive and the rights and wrongs according to Molloy are valuable to know. You can also find magazine and newspaper articles on the subject. Although they, too, are filled with subjective opinions, they'll help increase your awareness. Then you can fit your own style and taste into the general principles.

7. Ask How You Look

The simplest way to get immediate feedback is to ask others, for example, "How does this look?" Although people are sensitive to your feelings, if you're continually open and forthright, you'll gain a valuable perspective on yourself. Don't be shy. Others will soon realize you're serious and give you their honest opinions. If you act on the valid opinions you receive, your dress and appearance will become more and more effective.

DRESS AND APPEARANCE
PERSONAL GOAL WORKSHEET

Determine your answer to each question below and check Y for yes or N for no. You may not yet know your own communication skills well enough to answer every question, but review the book regularly until you can.

	Y	N
1. Have you tried wearing your hair a different way—parted on the other side, or frizzed, permed, crew-cut, sprayed, or tinted?	❑	❑
2. Do your glasses inhibit good eye communication?	❑	❑
3. Have you tried glasses vs. contact lenses? Is there a difference in effectiveness?	❑	❑
4. Do you organize the clothes in your closet by design?	❑	❑
5. Do people notice your jewelry?	❑	❑
6. Are people distracted by your jewelry?	❑	❑
7. Do you ever dress to shock people, or for effect, or for any reason other than to cover your body?	❑	❑
8. Are you always aware of your grooming? (For example, are your nails trimmed and clean? Do you bathe daily? Are your clothes always clean and pressed?)	❑	❑

CONTINUED

List three habitual patterns in your dress and appearance that you want to modify, strengthen, or eliminate:

1. _____

_____

2. _____

_____

3. _____

_____

Then write what you plan to practice to modify, strengthen, or change each habit.

1. _____

_____

2. _____

_____

3. _____

_____

Remember: Practice Makes Permanent

Language, Nonwords, and Pauses

Perhaps of all of the creations of man, language is the most astonishing."

–Lytton Strachey

Language is made of both words and nonwords. People communicate most effectively when they're able to select the right words. Doing so requires a rich vocabulary that can be used responsively and appropriately, as the situation demands. You wouldn't talk to a child the same way you'd to a group of physicists.

Pauses are an integral part of language. An effective communicator uses natural pauses between sentences, and outstanding communicators pause for dramatic effect as well. Nonword fillers—such as *um*, *ah*, *er*, *well*, *okay*, and *you know*—are barriers to clear communication.

Behavioral Objective

Your goal in developing your language skills is to *use appropriate and clear language for your listeners*. Work to *replace* irritating, distracting, and undermining nonwords with pauses. Pauses enable you to gather your thoughts and allow your listeners to think about what you're saying.

Keys to Effective Use of Language and Pauses

The more you build your communication skills, the more aware you become of the importance of the words—or nonwords—you use. The following tips will help you improve your use of language:

▶ **Use Direct Language**

State and ask for what you want and mean. In her book, *Customer Satisfaction: Practical Tools for Building Important Relationships*, Dru Scott emphasizes the difference between direct and indirect language by recommending you replace "I'll try" with "I will" and "We can't" with "You can." Rather than saying, "I'll try and get an answer for you," replace it with "I will check and get back to you before 4 P.M."

▶ **Increase Your Vocabulary**

Children increase their vocabulary through formal study at school. As adults, we don't have the same motivation, because we aren't being directly graded. But our educational level, clarity, and effectiveness in communications are "graded" daily by the words we use. All of us can increase our vocabulary through the active incorporation of new words.

▶ **Beware of Jargon**

Jargon is excellent communication shorthand for people who share an occupation or group membership. But even English words sound like a foreign language if your listener is outside that group and doesn't understand your jargon.

▶ **Incorporate More Pauses**

You can pause naturally for three to four seconds, even in the middle of a sentence. The problem is we aren't used to doing it. In our own minds, a three- or four-second pause can seem like 20 seconds. Practice pausing and getting feedback to learn how natural you sound when you pause. Push pausing to the limit during practice and you'll do it more naturally in real conversations.

▶ **Replace Nonwords with Pauses**

Some people call them "word whiskers"—fillers such as *um, ah, er, well, okay*, and *you know* that are unwanted and superfluous barriers to communication. Such nonwords aren't only sloppy but also distracting when repeated as a habit. Record yourself or solicit feedback to recognize your nonwords, and then concentrate to eliminate them.

Examples: Language, Nonwords, and Pauses

▶ Toni is the executive housekeeper of a major hotel chain. She's a big woman with a resonant voice and a confident air. When she talks, she ends every other sentence with "Okay?" Her habit of "asking for agreement" is inconsistent with her natural confidence and the content of her message.

▶ A major government official made a three-minute, eleven-second statement justifying an attack on an enemy position. In that short period, there were 57 "um's," "er's," and "ah's." The credibility of his statement was dramatically flawed with these nonword fillers of nervousness.

▶ Kevin is an outstanding speech trainer. At six feet, six inches tall with a booming voice, he's good looking, articulate, and much in demand as a speaker. He also has one distraction. In conversation (as well as in speeches), he often inserts the word "sort of" as a qualifier. This diminishes his credibility, particularly when he's making an emphatic statement. Such qualifiers are ingrained habits that are difficult to break.

Do you see yourself in these examples? If so, there's hope. You can improve your use of language, nonwords and pauses by practicing the following suggestions and exercises.

Improving Your Use of Language and Pauses

Listed below are several skill development exercises and tips to enhance your use of language and pauses in the dozens of interpersonal communications you have daily.

1. **Use One New Word a Day**

   Force yourself to use a new word every day in conversation. Find a half dozen times to use that word. Try words such as *dissemble, jocular, fulsome, empirical, robust,* and *espouse.* The words do not have to be long or intellectual—just different. Make your own list and work at it daily.

2. **Use a Dictionary**

   Keep a dictionary at your desk at work and at home—and use it. Most of us rarely use a dictionary unless it becomes a habit. Just looking up each new word you read or hear will increase your vocabulary. A larger vocabulary gives you the ability to draw on the right word or phrase when appropriate. It doesn't mean you use big words to show off—simply that you're able to use the clearest, most colorful, most apt word for the situation.

3. **Watch Your Jargon**

   We all have some jargon in our lives. List ten jargon phrases common to you. Make yourself aware when you use them. It's fine to use them with people who understand what they mean, but they can be alienating or confusing to others.

4. **Incorporate Pauses**

   Speak into a recorder and consciously leave pauses. At first, leave a three-second pause between sentences. Then leave a three- or four-second pause in the middle of a sentence. Exaggerate the pauses so they feel very long while recording them. Then on playback, listen to how natural they sound.

5. **Get Rid of Your Nonwords**

   Get rid of nonword fillers using two simple ways to modify your behavior:

   a. Ask an associate or friend to say your name every time you use your habitual nonword. For example, if you tend to use "um," ask your partner simply to state your name every time you say "um" in a conversation. He should do this without saying anything else. Your name is simply a feedback tool. You'll quickly become sensitized to your use of that nonword. Before long, your mind will stop you before you say it, and you'll leave a pause as a replacement.

   b. Record yourself at every opportunity to sensitize yourself to your nonword. Listening to it over and over will remind you to leave a pause instead of the irritating, distracting nonword that you use. Record yourself just chatting or in formal situations or on the phone—it doesn't matter. Just be sure to continue the feedback daily.

LANGUAGE, NONWORDS, AND PAUSES
PERSONAL GOAL WORKSHEET

Determine your answer to each question below and check Y for yes or N for no. You may not yet know your own communication skills well enough to answer every question, but review the book regularly until you can.

		Y	N
1.	Do you know how long you pause when you're speaking formally?	❑	❑
2.	Does your occupation use jargon?	❑	❑
3.	Do you use slang, code words, or jargon in your normal conversation without realizing it?	❑	❑
4.	Can you recall the last time you looked up a new word in the dictionary?	❑	❑
5.	Do you know the appropriate length of a pause?	❑	❑
6.	Do you use pauses automatically?	❑	❑
7.	Are you able to pause for dramatic effect?	❑	❑
8.	Do you know what the most common nonword is?	❑	❑

CONTINUED

List three habitual patterns in your use of language, nonwords, and pauses that you want to modify, strengthen, or eliminate:

1. _____
   _____

2. _____
   _____

3. _____
   _____

Then write what you plan to practice to modify, strengthen, or change each habit.

1. _____
   _____

2. _____
   _____

3. _____
   _____

Remember: Practice Makes Permanent

Part Summary

In this part, you learned how to **develop credibility**. You learned how to use **dress** and **appearance** to look appropriate to your environment. Then, you learned how to use **language**, **nonwords**, and **pauses** to create appropriate and clear language for your listeners, and to replace distracting nonwords with pauses.

Developing
Interaction

"_Well done is better than well said._"

–Benjamin Franklin

In this part:

- ▶ Developing Interaction
- ▶ Listener Involvement
- ▶ Humor
- ▶ The Natural Self

Developing Interaction

Once you've established **connection**, **energy** and **credibility**, your final objective is to develop **interaction** with your listeners. In this chapter we target the behavioral skills of:

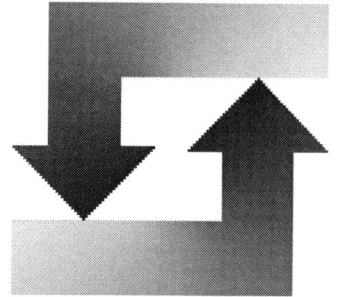

▶ Listener involvement

▶ Humor

▶ The natural self.

Remember that your audience can be one person or a thousand. The more you interact, the more engaged your listener is and the more effective and skilled you'll be in making an impact as a leader.

Listener involvement can be cultivated in many ways, all of which entail the listener engaging his or her own mind in your communication. This involvement can result from a question, doing an exercise, filling in a blank, or even a mental image you inspire in the mind of your listener.

People relate to people they like. We relate to one another when we engage and interact. To develop interaction with our listener, we must hone in on the behavioral skills that contribute to such engaged interaction: *Listener Involvement, Humor*, and *The Natural Self.*

Listener Involvement

Your listeners won't care what you say until they know that you care."

—**Anonymous**

When you speak and engage a listener at the intellectual level only, you're operating in a narrow range. You're appealing mostly to the linear processing of the left brain. For pure information, this is adequate. Then again, facts and figures can be communicated effectively in writing. Indeed, people can read five times faster than you can speak.

Communicating interpersonally, on the other hand, involves ideas and opinions. You're trying to move people to action or persuade them to agree. If you miss engaging your listeners' right brains, you're missing much of your potential for impact.

Behavioral Objective

Your goal in developing your listener involvement skills is to *maintain the active interest of each person with whom you're communicating*, every time you talk— whether to one person or a thousand.

Keys to Effective Listener Involvement Skills

Whether just one person in a conversation or many people in an audience, listeners are bombarded by stimuli every instant. You must engage all of the senses and all of the mind. The more involved your listeners are, the more you can convince them of your message.

Engaging Listeners with "Swirls"

A "swirl" is an instant of a listener's total involvement. A swirl can come from laughing, sensing an "aha" moment, being invited to the front to do an exercise, having to think of a question, deciding whether to volunteer, and the like.

Many swirls are created through humor and humanization, but they can come from any of the *nine listener-involving techniques* listed below. The nine techniques center around three areas: style, interaction, and content, as follows:

Style	Interaction	Content
Drama	Questions	Interest
Eye Communication	Demonstrations	Humor
Movement	Samples/Gimmicks	
Visuals		

All of these techniques can be adapted to large groups or to individual communication.

Improving Your Listener Involvement

As a speaker, your action to involve your listeners could be as slight as moving into the audience or using a different type of visual aid. Or you could do something more substantial, as in the following examples.

Drama

▶ Create a strong opening by announcing a serious problem, telling a moving story, or asking a rhetorical question to get each person thinking. You can also make a startling statement.

▶ Include a dramatic element, such as a long pause, to emphasize a key statement, vocal tone and pitch changes, or higher-intensity emotions, such as anger, joy, sadness, or excitement.

▶ Add visual and kinesthetic detail, such as color, smell, temperature, and other sensations, to recreate a story or experience vividly for your listeners.

▶ End your communication with a dramatic or inspirational quote or a firm call to action.

Eye Communication

▶ Survey all of your listeners when you start speaking before beginning extended eye communication with any individual.

▶ Keep your listeners involved and engaged by maintaining three- to six-second contact with as many as possible. Don't forget the "orphans" at the far edges of a room or along your side of a conference table.

▶ Gauge the reaction of your listeners throughout your presentation. Do they agree? Are they bored? Do they have questions?

Movement

▶ Change the dynamics of your presentation with purposeful movement. Whenever possible, move around.

▶ Never back away from your listeners. Move toward them—especially at the beginning and the end of your communication.

Visuals

▶ Add variety by using visuals. Give your listeners something to look at in addition to you.

▶ Use various types of visual aids in a formal presentation, such as overheads and flip charts. Rehearse to make your transitions smooth and non-distracting.

▶ Get on-the-spot listener participation by experimenting with techniques such as writing listener concerns on a flip chart or filling in an overhead transparency as you go.

LISTENER INVOLVEMENT
PERSONAL GOAL WORKSHEET

Determine your answer to each question below and check Y for yes or N for no. You may not yet know your own communication skills well enough to answer every question, but review the book regularly until you can.

		Y	N
1.	Do you know the three different forms of questions?	☐	☐
2.	Do you physically move around when you're in a speaking situation?	☐	☐
3.	Are you aware of the need to engage your audience's right brain?	☐	☐
4.	If you're presenting a lot of information, do you obtain regular feedback signals by involving your audience?	☐	☐

Now list two habitual patterns in your listener involvement skills that you want to modify, strengthen, or eliminate:

1. _____

   _____

2. _____

   _____

Then write what you plan to practice to modify, strengthen, or change each habit.

1. _____

   _____

2. _____

   _____

Remember: Practice Makes Permanent

Humor

> " *The man who causes them to laugh gets more votes for the measure than the man who forces them to think.*"
>
> **– Malcolm de Chazall**

Humor is one of the most important skills for effective interpersonal communication, yet one of the most elusive. Some people are naturally personable and likable. Others have to work at it. Humor is a learnable skill that we can all learn to use more effectively.

Behavioral Objective

Your goal in developing your humor skills is to *create a bond between yourself and your listeners*. Your use of humor enables them to enjoy listening to you more. Humor can make you more "human" and help others have a good time when they're around you.

Keys to the Effective Use of Humor

Some of the most effective swirls come from moments of lightness or involvement. Those emotional moments are the best time to get your message through. You reach both the right brain and the left brain when you use humor and humanization. The following tips will help you develop your use of humor:

▶ **Don't Tell Jokes**

About one in 100 persons is a good teller of jokes, but ten times that number think they can tell jokes well. Unless you're really effective at pacing, delivery, and style, don't try telling jokes in formal situations.

▶ **Do Tell Stories and Anecdotes**

We're funny, humorous, and human when we open ourselves to be vulnerable—to be part of the human comedy. Much can be gained in interpersonal communications by sharing humorous asides, stories, anecdotes, and reactions.

▶ **Humanization Is Humor**

In most interpersonal communications, comedy isn't really the goal. Instead, we want to connect on the personal level with our listeners. That connection is most often made through likeability. This quality comes from such factors as being personal, open, friendly, caring, interested, personable, emotional, concerned, pleasant, comfortable, confident, unselfish, feeling, and fun.

▶ **Remember the Personality Factor**

People often vote for political leaders on the basis of likeability. Others decide whether they agree with you or support your position based on personality. Both factors are most characterized by the humor or humanization that you project.

▶ **Your Smile Is What People See**

When we're talking, people look at our faces. Our predominant feature is our smiles. This important feature shows quickly whether we're excited, enthused, angry, serious, or some combination of these. Our sense of humor is largely perceived nonverbally through a smile. It's important to know your natural "smileability."

Improving Your Use of Humor

Listed below are several skill development exercises and tips to enhance your use of humor in the dozens of interpersonal communications you have daily.

1. **Determine What Makes You Laugh**

   Find out more about your sense of humor. Do you have a dry wit, or do you like earthy stories? Do you have an infectious laugh, or do you exhibit an easy smile? Everybody's different, yet most of us love to laugh and have fun. Find out what your "humor profile" is by asking others to rate your sense of humor on a scale of one to ten.

2. **Make Someone Else Laugh**

   People can consciously use humor. In a few seconds, one person can make another person (or a group of people) laugh, smile, chuckle, chortle, or relax—if they work at it. If you make humor a conscious goal, then with everything that passes through your mind, you'll automatically look for the connection that relates to the human comedy.

3. **Think Funny**

   People who laugh easily tend to filter their world through a screen of humor. Theirs is a brighter, lighter side perspective. They can turn a crisis into an opportunity. Think funny on a conscious level. You'll be surprised at how this conscious effort enables you to be more spontaneous, open, and fun.

4. **Gain Awareness through Feedback**

   Record every formal presentation you give. Use humor in your talk and then check the audience feedback to see how it worked. Count the laughs, chuckles, and smiles that you're able to generate from your audience.

5. **Watch Others**

   We all know people we enjoy being around. We want to be with them, because they're fun, light, and lively. Search these people out. See how they involve others. Experiment with trying some of their habits and adapting those habits to your style.

6. **Keep a Humor Journal**

   In a journal or diary, keep a page for quotes, quips, anecdotes, stories, and funny things that happen in your daily life. Do this for a week, noting ten light items in your life each day. If you don't have ten a day, work harder at humor. Life is meant to be joyful.

HUMOR
PERSONAL GOAL WORKSHEET

Determine your answer to each question below and check Y for yes or N for no. You may not yet know your own communication skills well enough to answer every question, but review the book regularly until you can.

	Y	N
1. Are you funny? Do you laugh at yourself?	☐	☐
2. Do you know the estimated percentage of people who know how to tell jokes well?	☐	☐
3. Do you tell more than two jokes a week?	☐	☐
4. Do people tend to laugh when they're around you?	☐	☐
5. Do you know what makes you laugh?	☐	☐

Now list two habitual patterns in your humor skills that you want to modify, strengthen, or eliminate:

1. _____

_____

2. _____

_____

Then write what you plan to practice to modify, strengthen, or change each habit.

1. _____

_____

2. _____

_____

The Natural Self

> **"** *When we encounter a natural style, we are always surprised and delighted, for we thought to see an author and found a man.* "
>
> **–Pascal**

Think of the most forceful speaker you know. Think of the most impressive leader you know. In each case, you won't find one who's a copy of anybody else. We're each different—each with our own strengths and weaknesses. Although this is a simple concept, it gains complexity when you consider the thousands of variables in interpersonal communications. We have resources to draw on—natural strengths that are already there—as well as areas to make into strengths.

Behavioral Objective

Your goal in developing your natural self is to *be authentic*. Work to be yourself in all communication circumstances, understanding and using your natural strengths and building communication weaknesses into strengths. To be your natural self, have the confidence in your mental spontaneity to adapt to circumstances.

Keys to Being Your Natural Self

Being your natural self is an attitude that involves (1) acknowledging your strengths and your weak areas, and (2) converting your weaknesses into strengths. It's as much a behavioral skill as the eight covered already (Eye Communication, Posture and Movement, Gestures and Facial Expressions, Dress and Appearance, Voice and Vocal Variety, Language, Nonwords, and Pauses, and Humor).

Learning like a Juggler

If you ever learned to juggle, you probably learned to start with one ball first just to get the rhythm. Then you added a second ball to practice with both hands working together. Finally, you practiced adding a third ball until you could juggle.

Becoming an expert in interpersonal communications is much like juggling. You master one skill at a time and add to them once they become habits.

A good start is to acknowledge your natural strengths and be thankful you don't have to learn them from scratch. Realize that many others don't have what you have. You may have an easy, natural smile while others have to work at lightening up in their interpersonal communications. On the other hand, you may find it difficult to gesture naturally, while someone else might have been born effusive. Acknowledge your strengths and work to improve and capitalize on them.

Next, work on your weaknesses, one at a time, until you convert them into strengths. Take your weakest area first and concentrate on improving it every day for a week. For example, if eye communication is a difficult skill for you, put your conscious mental energy into developing extended eye communication each day for a week or two. Then move to another skill. Continue this process until you've gone through all nine skills.

Communicating Well Is a Lifetime Process

No one is a completed, effective communicator. We always find new unwanted habits that pop up, as well as old undesirable habits that creep back. We also find new strengths as we mature and as we experiment with various behavioral skills.

Often a newfound habit works to improve an old habit. Or two habits work together to form an effective new behavior. For example, movement and extended eye communication can breed confidence that allows a person to maintain excellent eye communication with a listener. It may even allow reaching out and touching the listener's arm.

Remember that interpersonal communication involves a multitude of skills. And all skills can be learned and practiced.

Discovering Your Natural Self

Listed below are two skill development exercises and tips for helping you analyze your strengths and weaknesses and find out if your analysis matches others' impressions of you.

Ask 5 people…

Show five people the list of the nine behavioral skills and ask each person to rank you, from your greatest strength to your greatest weakness. Observe what others see in you. Compare the responses with your self-perceptions. If they match, you know where to start work. If they don't, take those areas that are least consistent and work on them first.

Ask 3 people…

Ask three people to fill out in detail a Coaching Feedback Sheet (such as the one on the next page) about you after your next presentation.

COACHING FEEDBACK SHEET

	Excellent	Good	Needs Work	Comments
Overall Impression				
Appearance				
Enthusiasm				
Posture				
Expressions				
Content				
Opening				
Listener Involvement				
Word Pictures				
Examples/Quotes				
Lack of Jargon				
Closing				
Delivery Skills				
Extended Eye Contact				
Natural Gestures				
Use of Nonwords				
Pauses				
Voice				
Natural Movement				
Humor				
Visual Aids				
Overall Impression				
Appearance				
Enthusiasm				

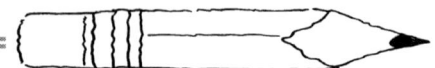

NATURAL SELF
PERSONAL GOAL WORKSHEET

Determine your answer to each question below and check Y for yes or N for no. You may not yet know your own communication skills well enough to answer every question, but review the book regularly until you can.

	Y	N
1. Are you comfortable speaking in any of these situations: to a small group, to a large audience, in a high-pressure one-on-one sales situation?	❏	❏
2. Do you know in which of the four stages of speaking you normally reside?	❏	❏
3. Do you know what behavioral changes you experience during high-stress communications?	❏	❏
4. Do you know your three strongest communication skill areas?	❏	❏
5. What about your three weakest?	❏	❏

Now list two habitual patterns identified in your natural self that you want to modify, strengthen, or eliminate:

1. _____

   _____

2. _____

   _____

Then write what you plan to practice to modify, strengthen, or change each habit.

1. _____

   _____

2. _____

   _____

Part Summary

In this part, you learned how to **develop interaction**. You learned how to use **listener involvement** to maintain the interest of each person with whom you're communicating. Next, you learned how to use **humor** to create a bond between yourself and your listeners. Finally, you learned how to use **the natural self** to be authentic, to have confidence to adapt to circumstances.

Creating a Communication Experience

Think of communication not as an interaction, but as an experience you have with another person or a group of people. As you develop your behavioral skills for more interpersonal effectiveness, the changes you make in your communication habits are likely to have an impact—a positive one.

What can you do to create an experience with another person or a group? Apply these tips:

▶ **Exhibit confident behavior.** Without expressing confidence in your interactions, all else will be lost.

▶ **Put yourself in their shoes.** What will stand out for them in the interaction? What's in it for them if they have a positive experience?

▶ **Think *story*.**[1] We all love to hear a story, and we relate to stories by experiencing them. Use stories in your communications. Use word pictures, metaphors, props, and quotes. Make your communications live and breathe.

▶ **Think of the senses.** All five senses connect to the first brain. The visual and auditory are most dominant, so use them with great expression to allow your listener to experience you. And when you can, go beyond to the other senses—touch, taste, and smell. Doing so requires more creativity, but you can do it. (For example, if you have a small office, have chocolate chip cookies for your clients. Meet over a meal rather than in your office. For a speech, have candy on the chairs. Shake hands warmly with two hands rather than with one.)

▶ **Expand your framework** to enlarge the communication experience.

---

[1] For more information on communicating through stories, read *Making Your Message Memorable* by Deborah Shouse, Ron Zoglin, and Susan Fenner, Ph.D.

Influencing Others through Six Leadership Skills

Great leaders are great communicators, and great communicators can become leaders in their own spheres of influence. Through communicating effectively, leaders are able to exert influence.

There are six skills of leadership that can be learned and improved with intention and practice. All are related to how we communicate and relate to others. Three of them specifically depend on the ability to communicate effectively.

Mastering the following six skills will put you in the mindset of a leader and set you up for success and influence:

Individual Characteristics

Leaders have and look for:

▶ Forward leaning—Leaders are communicators. Their energy and people skills enable them to exert influence.

▶ Character—Leaders have ethics, integrity, trustworthiness, and humility. Leaders care and consider the organization first. Leaders aren't sarcastic.

▶ Savvy—Leaders are intelligent, street-smart, conceptual, and tactical. They have an entrepreneurial spirit, and they're good managers.

Team (Organization, Group) Actions

Leaders do the following:

▶ Communicate a clear vision—Leaders are passionate about where they want the group to go, and they continually articulate and repeat the vision—up, down, and laterally.

▶ Mobilize resources—Leaders know what they need to get the job done through others, and they continually assemble and motivate the resources required.

▶ Manage (self and others) through measurements—What you measure is what you get. Leaders manage themselves first by high and specific standards and motivate others through measurements.

Review: The 9 Behavioral Skills for Effective Interpersonal Communication

Vocal delivery and the visual elements, as well as personality, likeability, and openness are the primary ingredients of communication skills for leaders.

For your review, the specific behavioral characteristics and traits that make up these important ingredients are the following:

1. Eye Communication: to look sincerely and steadily at another person

2. Posture and Movement: to stand tall and move naturally and easily

3. Gestures and Facial Expressions: to be relaxed and natural when you speak

4. Voice and Vocal Variety: to use your voice as a rich, resonant instrument.

5. Dress and Appearance: to dress, groom, and appear appropriate for the environment you're in, as well as for yourself

6. Language, Nonwords, and Pauses: to use appropriate and clear language for your listeners, replacing nonwords with pauses

7. Listener Involvement: to maintain the active interest and involvement of each person with whom you're communicating

8. Using Humor: to create a bond between yourself and your listeners

9. The Natural Self: to be authentic

Communicating is a learnable skill. It takes work, but the results are worth it. With practice, you can raise this skill to an art form, and even enjoy the process.

Remember, Practice Makes Permanent!

Appendix to Part 1

Comments & Suggested Responses

Believability Broken Down

Professor Mehrabian's results:

Dominant Believability Elements	
Verbal	7%
Vocal	38%
Visual	55%

Additional Reading

50-Minute Manager Series books:

Bozek, Phillip. *50 One-Minute Tips to Better Communication.*

Chapman, Elwood N. and Wil McKnight. *Attitude.*

Kravitz, S. Michael and Susan D. Schubert. *Emotional Intelligence Works.*

Manning, Marilyn and Patricia Haddock. *Developing as a Professional.*

Other related reading:

Decker, Bert. *Creating Messages That Motivate.* San Francisco: Just Write Books, 2005.

Decker, Bert. *You've Got To Be Believed To Be Heard.* NY: St. Martin's Press, 1992.

Gladwell, Malcolm. *Blink.* NY: Little, Brown and Company, 2005.

Goleman, Daniel. *Emotional Intelligence.* NY: Bantam, 1997.

Goleman, Daniel, Richard Boyatzis, and Annie McKee. *Primal Leadership.* Boston, MA: Harvard Business School Press, 2002.

Lencioni, Patrick. *Death by Meeting.* San Francisco: Jossey-Bass, 2004.

Also Available

If you enjoyed this book, we have great news for you. There are over 150 books available in the **50-Minute Manager™ Series.** For more information visit us online at 50minutemanager.com

Subject Areas Include:

Accounting & Finance
Business Ethics
Business Skills
Communication
Customer Service
Design
Diversity in Business
Human Resources & Leveraging Your People
Jobs & Careers
Management & Leadership
Operations
Product Development & Marketing
Sales Coaching & Prospecting
Women in Leadership
Writing & Editing

AX1424624886
ISBN-13 978-1-4246-2488-1
ISBN-10 1-4246-2488-6